Greater Than a Tourist
Lahore
Punjab
Pakistan

50 Travel Tips from a Local

Shehr Naz Ashraf

Copyright © 2017 CZYK Publishing
All Rights Reserved. No part of this publication may be reproduced, including scanning and photocopying, or distributed in any form or by any means, electronic or mechanical, or stored in a database or retrieval system without prior written permission from the publisher.

Disclaimer: The publisher has put forth an effort in preparing and arranging this book. The information provided herein by the author is provided "as is". Use this information at your own risk. Consult your doctor before engaging in any medical activities. The publisher and author disclaim any liabilities for any loss of profit or commercial or personal damages resulting from the information contained in this book.

Order Information: To order this title please email lbrenenc@gmail.com or visit GreaterThanATourist.com. A bulk discount can be provided.

Cover Template Creator: Lisa Rusczyk Ed. D. using Canva.
Cover Creator: Lisa Rusczyk Ed. D.
Image: https://pixabay.com/en/lahore-lahore-city-lhr-2299773/

CZYK
PUBLISHING

Lock Haven, PA
All rights reserved.
ISBN: 9781549881985

>TOURIST

Shehr Naz Ashraf

BOOK DESCRIPTION

Are you excited about planning your next trip?

Do you want to try something new?

Would you like some guidance from a local?

If you answered yes to any of these questions, then this Greater Than a Tourist book is for you.

Greater Than a Tourist – Lahore, Pakistan by Shehr Naz Ashraf offers the inside scoop on Lahore. Most travel books tell you how to sightsee. Although there's nothing wrong with that, as a part of the Greater than a Tourist series, this book will give you tips from someone who lives at your next travel destination. In these pages, you'll discover local advice that will help you throughout your trip. Travel like a local. Slow down and get to know the people and the culture of a place. By the time you finish this book, you will be eager and prepared to travel to your next destination.

Shehr Naz Ashraf

TABLE OF CONTENTS

BOOK DESCRIPTION

TABLE OF CONTENTS

DEDICATION

ABOUT THE AUTHOR

HOW TO USE THIS BOOK

FROM THE PUBLISHER

WELCOME TO > TOURIST

INTRODUCTION

1. Begin Your Journey With A Visit To The Minar-e-Pakistan

2. Get Used To Lahoris Saying, "L'hore, L'hore Aye!"

3. The First Heritage Site On Your To-Visit List Has To Be The Lahore Fort

4. Don't Fuss About Your Weight When In Lahore; You Are Bound To Put On Some Pounds!

5. Pay A Visit To Old Lahore

6. Explore Lahore's Most Prestigious Museums

7. Appreciate The Sufi Influence In Lahore

8. Don't Forget To Visit Cooco's Den

9. When Craving City-Feels, Head To Shopping Malls

10. Run Down A Pictorial History Of Lahore At The Tollinton Market

11. Travel At Least Once On The Metrobus

12. You Can't Miss Khalifa's Nankhatai

13. Experience The Daily Ceremony At Wagah Border At Least Once

14. Join The Rafi Peer Theatre Workshop's Performing Arts' Festivals

15. Prepare To Be Met With "Lights" Everywhere

16. Get Acquainted With Pakistan's Struggle For Independence At The Army Museum

17. Spend An Evening At Salt'N Pepper Village

18. Get Sporty At The Battlefield

19. Try A Classic Cone At Paradise

20. Catch A Pleasant Breeze At The Shalimar Gardens

21. Don't Hold Back On Your Humor

22. Have A Chill Lassi At Chacha Feeka Lassi To Brighten Up Your Day

23. Become A Part Of The Horse And Cattle Show At Fortress Stadium
24. Experience A Throwback Into Mughal Glory At Jahangir's Tomb
25. Drive Along The Canal Bank Road
26. Enjoy Lahore's Nightlife At Liberty Market
27. Try Nisbat Gol Gappay For A Mouthwatering Snack
28. Sit With Lahoris During Cricket Matches
29. Have A Movie Night At CineStar IMAX
30. Spend A Lazy Day At The Jilani Park
31. Bond With Wildlife At The Lahore Zoo
32. Switch Your Omelet Up For A Halwa Puri Breakfast At Taj Mahal Sweets
33. Visit The National Museum Of Science And Technology For An Educational Experience
34. Visit Lahore's Very Own Eiffel Tower
35. Shop Like A Lahori At Anarkali Bazaar
36. If You Happen To Visit Lahore During Eid Holidays, Then Don't Even Think Of Sitting Back Home
37. Do Get A Taste Of Paan

38. While Driving, Take A Moment To Check Out The Artistic Development On Roads

39. Ditch Taxis For Auto-rickshaws And Qingqis

40. Watch A Live Cricket Match At Gaddafi Stadium

41. Get Intellectual At The Lahore Literary Festival

42. Don't Deprive Yourself Of Phajjay Ke Paye

43. Get Thrilled At Joyland

44. For The Cheapest Rates, Visit Kareem Block Market

45. Fly Through Lahore's Skies With The Lahore Flying Club

46. Don't Leave Out The Javed Manzil When Visiting Lahore

47. Check Out Kamran's Baradari At The Shahdara Bagh

48. Stop By The Grand Jamia Masjid At Bahria Town To View Extraordinary Splendor

49. Free Your Soul At The Mela Chiraghan

50. Elders Who Tell Stories Are A Definite Source Of Entertainment

Top Reasons to Book This Trip

Our Story

Notes

DEDICATION

This book is dedicated to my mother, Kushaf Sarwar, who has raised me to be a Lahori by heritage, but a human by heart.

Shehr Naz Ashraf

ABOUT THE AUTHOR

Shehr Naz Ashraf is a knowledge-hungry girl who lives in Lahore, Pakistan. She likes to read and write when her creative spurts kick in. Traveling to places that divert from mainstream trends and help her bust stereotypes about people, places, and cultures is a hobby of hers. From very early on, Shehr Naz gained recognition for her creative essays at school, which ultimately evolved into a passion for writing.

Shehr Naz has lived in Lahore since birth. She is a typical and true, born and bred Lahori and stays true to her roots. Her fifteen plus years at Lahore define her as a local.

Shehr Naz Ashraf

HOW TO USE THIS BOOK

The Greater Than a Tourist book series was written by someone who has lived in an area for over three months. The goal of this book is to help travelers either dream or experience different locations by providing opinions from a local. The author has made suggestions based on their own experiences. Please do your own research before traveling to the area in case the suggested places are unavailable.

Shehr Naz Ashraf

FROM THE PUBLISHER

Traveling can be one of the most important parts of a person's life. The anticipation and memories that you have are some of the best. As a publisher of the Greater Than a Tourist book series, as well as the popular 50 Things to Know book series, we strive to help you learn about new places, spark your imagination, and inspire you. Wherever you are and whatever you do I wish you safe, fun, and inspiring travel.

Lisa Rusczyk Ed. D.

CZYK Publishing

Shehr Naz Ashraf

>TOURIST

WELCOME TO > TOURIST

Shehr Naz Ashraf

INTRODUCTION

Greater Than a Tourist – Lahore, Pakistan will guide you to travel and explore Lahore fully, the way only a local could. The book aims to correct the perspectives of travelers who have been prompted by international media to believe that all of Pakistan is a breeding ground for terrorism. Lahore is and has been home to the subcontinent's most renowned saints, poets and kings of magnificent empires. Lahore holds the deepest of literature, the liveliest of artwork and the most intricate of architecture. We Lahoris are people of bliss and extravagance, sugar and spice, and romance and tragedy. The blend of the past and the present here makes the city truly unique.

Hopefully, you will be able to grasp Lahore's true colors of hospitality and humor and enjoy your stay in Lahore with all your being. Happy Reading!

Shehr Naz Ashraf

1. Begin Your Journey With A Visit To The Minar-e-Pakistan

The Minar-e-Pakistan (literally the 'Tower of Pakistan') would be a wise place to initiate your journey through Lahore. Constructed in 1968, the monument commemorates the passing of the Pakistan Resolution on March 23, 1940 – the first official demand for an independent and separate state for the Muslims of Hindustan. Four platforms form the base of the tower and the material of the platforms becomes finer as they ascend, with the lowest level made from uncut stones and the highest level made of polished white marble. This depicts the ladder of the success of the Pakistan Movement. The 203-feet-high tower is an essential landmark of Lahore that serves as the location for a number of important events and holidays. An elevator takes you up to the top of the tower to experience the panoramic view of the tower itself and its surrounding grand structures like the Badshahi Mosque. The beautiful Mughal influences, the tomb of Hafeez Jalandhari (writer of Pakistan's national anthem) and the inscriptions on the pillars are noteworthy features of the Minar-e-Pakistan. As a local, I recommend visiting the place on national or religious holidays like Eid Milad-un-Nabi or the Independence Day. The tower is lit up in brilliant lights and a firework display completes the picture-perfect view. Colorful dancing fountains, as well as buggy rides, are popular attractions for many. Leaving out this monument on your visit to Lahore is a disgrace; the Minar-e-Pakistan is the Pride of Pakistan.

2. Get Used To Lahoris Saying, "L'hore, L'hore Aye!"

If there was an award for the most overused phrase of all-time, "L'hore, L'hore Aye!" would surely win first place. The phrase isn't a very deep quote or some mystical spell but has a rather simple meaning. It literally means 'Lahore is Lahore'. So why exactly is it always incorporated into Lahoris' daily speech? Simply because we Lahoris take pride in being from Lahore and we want to emphasize Lahore's unique and special self! There is no city like Lahore in all of South Asia. Cultural capital, best food in town and the closest thing to a hub in Pakistan: that's the Lahore we are talking about! Call this conceit or arrogance all you want, but you have to admit – Lahore is just pure wonderful, right? Plus, this phrase is just half of the actual quote. The whole line goes, "L'hore, L'hore aye, jinnae L'hore ni waikhya o jamya e ni." This translates to, "Lahore is Lahore; you aren't born yet if you haven't seen Lahore."

Once you fully discover Lahore's treasures, I'm sure you'll be repeating the phrase too!

3. The First Heritage Site On Your To-Visit List Has To Be The Lahore Fort

The Lahore Fort is the unofficial trademark site of the city. If you were to ask a random person for sightseeing destinations in Lahore, the Lahore Fort would be the first place they would name. The twenty-acre-wide fortress holds an astonishing 21 notable sites that have undergone changes from the sixteenth till twentieth centuries, respectively under Mughal, Sikh and British rule. The Alamgiri Gate acts as the entrance to the grand fortress, leading to the most popular monument amongst those in the fort, the Badshahi Masjid. This iconic landmark has exquisitely carved red sandstone with white marble inlay and an interior beautified with intricate floral motifs; the place is indescribable, really. The unmatchable mirrored tile-work at the Sheesh Mahal (Palace of Mirrors) is next on the list. The palace in its entirety is embellished with convex glass, with the concept that the light of a single candle lit here would illuminate the whole palace, due to the reflection of the single beam. The massive Picture Wall, the breathtaking Moti Masjid (Pearl Mosque) and the iconic Naulakha Pavilion are just some of the many stunning monuments to visit at Lahore Fort. I would recommend heading to the fort early in the morning because it's going to take you an entire day, at the very least, to experience the grandeur of Mughal architecture.

4. Don't Fuss About Your Weight When In Lahore; You Are Bound To Put On Some Pounds!

In Pakistan, Lahore is synonymous with food. It is a known fact that Lahoris celebrate food like no other. Every street in Lahore has a place to eat. Restaurants, cafeterias, and diners are some of the most bustling businesses in Lahore. You can get delicious food at any price and any place, whether it's a tiny canteen in a park or a five-star hotel. The only difference in experience will be the setting and maintenance of the place. Open areas will have flies or little place to sit while five-star hotels will have air-conditioned halls and whole buffets. Yet food quality will be excellent almost everywhere. Moreover, you will find every type of cuisine in restaurants here, ranging from desi to Thai to Italian. The moral of the story is that you will eat like you have never eaten before. Gaining weight will be unavoidable once you land in Lahore. So don't worry about those numbers on the scales; they're just numbers! Besides, once you return to your homeland, you will surely miss all the foodie days you spent here. So gear up and eat to your heart's desire!

5. Pay A Visit To Old Lahore

Lahore may be a modernized metropolitan city, but it has an old and traditional side to it too. This part of Lahore is, to say the least, unmissable. Old Lahore, locally called Androon Shehar (Interior city) was composed of a city contained among thirteen huge gates. Of the thirteen, only six stand today; however, most of them are in deteriorated states. Once you enter through one of these gates, a whole new chapter of history and heritage opens up. The Wazir Khan Mosque is a must-see mosque with richly embellished frescoes and an intricately designed interior that will make you revisit the Mughal era. One should also visit its close associate, the Shahi Hammam, which contains a number of public baths and is quite a sight. The only light in the area is sunlight and the building is decorated in a number of Mughal era frescoes. The many havelis (mansions) are remnants of Mughal architecture, too. The area also has one of the biggest and best spice markets in the whole of South Asia; you will find various unique spices and mixtures here that belong exclusively to the Old City. If you're tired of all the walking around, then look for donkey-carts and rickshaws. The locals will give you a tour of the whole inner city on either of the two, which will make for a refreshing and therapeutic ride.

6. Explore Lahore's Most Prestigious Museums

A visit to any city in the world is incomplete if you don't visit its museums. Lahore's largest and most renowned museum is the Lahore Museum at Mall Road. This museum is also famous as the museum featured in Rudyard Kipling's novel Kim. The building itself is a wonderful piece of construction and holds artifacts and paintings dating back to the pre-historic times of the Indus Valley and Gandhara civilizations. The collection of 40,000 old Hellenistic and Mughal coins and rare manuscripts are known all over the world. An entire gallery is also dedicated to Pakistan's progress as an independent state. Do check out the collection of miniature paintings and the Gandhara Gallery's most famous relic: the Fasting Buddha. The Fakir Khana Museum in the Walled City should be another place to stop at if your quest for museums remains unfinished. This museum is the only government-recognized private museum of Pakistan, owned by the Fakir family and now being run by the sixth generation of the said family. The Hall of Miniatures containing a huge collection of miniature paintings and the portrait of Nawab Mumtaz Ali are the museum's main masterpieces. The Fakir Khana Museum is the largest private collection in all of South Asia, with over 13,000 relics. Each and every one of the collections is a spectacular reminder of the glorious past of the subcontinent.

7. Appreciate The Sufi Influence In Lahore

Look for signs of Sufism in everything pure and chaste. Lahore is located in Punjab, which was the center for the spread of Sufism in Pakistan. The place is filled with the shrines and tombs of renowned Sufis like Hazrat Data Ganj Baksh, Hazrat Mian Qadri, Madho Laal Hussain and much more. Shrines are the one place in Lahore that will always welcome everyone and anyone with open doors and will never be seen empty. If you get a chance to visit any of these shrines, you will find the influence of not religion, but love. The singing of mystical lores, people engaged in entranced dancing, the recitation of divine verses: all this will give you a heightening sense of peace. The best part about being in such places is that they hand out food at all times, and to literally anyone because here, everyone is equal. You will be mixed with locals and tourists, rich and poor and Muslims and non-Muslims. But one thing everyone will have in common is the serenenity that each and every person will possess and emit. A look into Sufism will definitely revitalize your spirits.

8. Don't Forget To Visit Cooco's Den

Cooco's Den is located on Fort Road Food Street, near the Roshnai Gate (one of the few surviving gates). It is the oldest building on the street and is frequented by most tourists. The restaurant offers the best of Pakistani cuisine, ranging from karahis and barbeque to daal and vegetable dishes. Not only is the food extremely scrumptious, but the restaurant's environment is also especially welcoming. Several musicians play harmonious tunes that will put anyone in awe. The road to Cooco's Den is marked with famous heritage sites like the Taxali Gate, Badshahi Masjid and some temples and churches. The restaurant itself is decorated with artifacts and paintings that speak volumes about Pakistan's history. But nothing beats the view from the top of the restaurant itself. Since the restaurant is located on the rooftop, it gives a breathtaking aerial view of the glorious Badshahi Mosque.

Cooco's Den opens at noon and closes an hour after midnight, but the best time to visit it is between evening and midnight. This is the time when the Badshahi Mosque's lights are switched on, so it makes for a stunning scene when viewed from the rooftop. You will probably have to clear up your camera's memory to make room for the heaps of photos you'll take at Cooco's Den!

9. When Craving City-Feels, Head To Shopping Malls

Shopping malls are the trend nowadays. Lahore did not have these many malls until a few years ago. Now that it does, everyone is flocking to these malls. The most notable ones are Mall of Lahore, Emporium Mall and Packages Mall. These three have a variety of brands and stores, with Emporium and Packages housing over two hundred plus brands. All three have huge floors dedicated to being food courts only. These malls have wide, air-conditioned and clean-swept halls. The best thing about them is that national and international brands both have outlets here and because of the intense competition of attracting more customers, sales and discounts are frequent schemes in stores. Not only can you choose from varieties of stores, but you can also get them at the best rates. Personally, I would place Packages Mall as a priority. The Mall has many fun-filled activities to offer as a plus, like a train that runs around the parking lot and a huge vintage car that you and your family/friends can ride around the first floor.

10. Run Down A Pictorial History Of Lahore At The Tollinton Market

The Tollinton Market is a place of nostalgic childhood memories for many Lahoris. The place has constantly evolved since 1864. From being an exhibition hall to becoming a market, the place is now part of the Lahore Heritage Museum, yet it is still addressed by its old name. It has been restored and transformed into elegant exhibition halls of an art gallery. The gallery primarily tells the history of Lahore through pictures and paintings and is an excellent way to learn about Lahore's history. This attraction on Mall Road is not a very time-consuming act, but it will help you in your entire stay throughout Lahore because most of Lahore's historical sites require some knowledge of the past in order to be able to fully value the glory of the structures.

"For we were not always burdened by debt, dependent on foreign aid and handouts; in the stories we tell of ourselves we were not the crazed and destitute radicals you see on your television channels but rather saints and poets and – yes – conquering kings. We built the Royal Mosque and the Shalimar Gardens in this city, and we built the Lahore Fort with its mighty walls and wide ramp for our battle-elephants. And we did these things when your country was still a collection of thirteen small colonies, gnawing away at the edge of a continent."

– Mohsin Hamid, The Reluctant Fundamentalist

Shehr Naz Ashraf

11. Travel At Least Once On The Metrobus

The Lahore Metrobus is Pakistan's first bus rapid transit system. The bus travels over a route twenty-seven kilometers long, of which eight kilometers are elevated. It connects various stops along Lahore's main artery, hence securing hundreds of passengers daily. The bus can be a bit crowded, especially during peak hours, but it is all worth the crowd. Single-ride tokens are as cheap as Rs.20 (approximately $0.19) and cost the same no matter what your destination is. The terminals have escalators and approach tubes with parking spaces that reduce the hassle of getting to the station itself. The buses are well-lit and air-conditioned, so the journey becomes easy and comfortable. On first thought, riding a bus might seem like the most mundane thing you could do in Lahore. But the Metrobus is a big deal for the people of Lahore. Riding it will give you a firsthand experience of Pakistan's road to becoming a developed country. The bus is a much modern and western system as compared to other schemes in Pakistan, so this experience will definitely stand out in a bunch of traditional practices.

12. You Can't Miss Khalifa's Nankhatai

If you visit Lahore and do not try Khalifa's nankhatai, most Lahoris would consider it an insult. Nankhatai is shortbread biscuits or cookies made up of flour, sugar and ghee or butter. Khalifa bakery is the most popular nankhatai bakery in the whole of Pakistan. The bakery is located on the far-off Lakar Mandi Bazar Road, but to make up for it, the bakery can deliver nankhatai straight to your houses. People all over from Pakistan come to Lahore just to get this sweet treat for their families. You can have either simple nankhatai or almond-flavored one. Either way, it tastes amazing. After trying it, you will definitely want to pack some to take back home to your family.

13. Experience The Daily Ceremony At Wagah Border At Least Once

The Wagah Border is the border that separates Pakistan from India. Getting to experience the flag-lowering ceremony, internationally called the Beating Retreats border ceremony, is a one of a kind opportunity. Soldiers from both countries collaborate and perform daily and attract numerous locals and tourists alike. Every evening before sunset, Pakistani and Indian soldiers parade simultaneously and end the parade with the lowering of the two nations' flags. While the flags are lowered, the huge iron gates at the border are opened. The flags are then folded up and followed by terse handshakes between soldiers from both sides, which finally leads to the closing of the gates. The ceremony is magnificent to watch because of the overwhelming sense of patriotism that soldiers from both sides exude. The whole process is a cross between brusqueness and respect. Overall, it is an awe-inspiring performance that will leave quite an impression on any spectator.

14. Join The Rafi Peer Theatre Workshop's Performing Arts' Festivals

Puppet shows, Sufi nights, dance performances – what is it that this cultural hub does not have? The Rafi Peer Theatre Workshop has been operating as a major cultural head of performing arts' events for more than thirty-five years now. The immensely popular World Performing Arts Festival, hosted by the said theatre, unites performing artists from over the globe for an eleven-day festival boasting over ninety shows in total. The workshop also holds Sufi nights, which feature the best of musicians and Sufi poets of the region. No matter what event is being held here during your visit to Lahore, you should attend it and experience the lively and colorful aura of Pakistani culture firsthand. The theatre is renowned for its wonderfully directed and executed puppet shows, which often garner large audiences. You can be a part of these too, especially since these shows are usually hosted in English.

15. Prepare To Be Met With "Lights" Everywhere

Lahore is often called the 'City of Lights'. That's because, in Lahore, you'll never find a dark road or an unlit street lamp. Where there is electricity, there is light. Street lights, phone torches, candles, you name it! Every single nook and cranny will be lit up and waiting to illuminate someone's path. This is part of what makes Lahore one of the liveliest cities you'll ever come across. Every lit up place houses an ongoing activity and because Lahoris are always up and awake at every hour, every place has some sort of bustle. The Canal even displays meticulously decorated figures lit up in various hues; this is only around August, though. The Model Town Park hosts a night of setting afloat lit-up lanterns in the sky, on the day before Independence Day. This makes for one of the most picturesque views you'll ever come across. Overall, you will come to love Lahore's bright and sparkling aura with a passion.

16. Get Acquainted With Pakistan's Struggle For Independence At The Army Museum

While most heritage sites will take you back to the Mughal era, not many will be reminiscent of the near-independence history. The struggles that Muslims faced before and after independence, the brave lives lost in this period and the recent war against terrorism are some of the highlights of the museum's contents. The Army Museum has been open to visits by the public since September 2017 and has since been frequented by masses, who wish to get a glimpse of Pakistan's political and military history. The Nishan-e-Haider gallery pays tribute to the eleven courageous soldiers who have had the honor of receiving the highest military gallantry award Pakistan has to offer. There are sections dedicated to Quaid-e-Azam (the founder of Pakistan) and the armed forces, with statues of prominent political figures from the past, including the Quaid himself, and military uniforms and other items that pay tribute to Pakistan's hardworking army. The place is bound to leave you in awe of the rich history of Pakistan.

17. Spend An Evening At Salt'N Pepper Village

If you're looking to eat strictly Pakistani cuisine in a strictly traditional Pakistani setting, then Salt'n Pepper Village, or Village for short, is the perfect place for you. This restaurant is a pride of Lahore, a place that has been visited by big names like the late Lady Diana and the late Prime

Minister Benazir Bhutto. The restaurant bears the concept of being a 'live buffet' where most of the food is cooked out front. The buffet has different menus for lunch, hi-tea, dinner and breakfast (Sundays only). Famous Lahori barbeque items like tikkas, all-time favorites like the magnificent nihari and delectable desserts like gulab jamuns are simply going to blow you away with their rich flavors and strong ambiance. The biggest impression, though, is left by the setting of the building. Right at the entrance stands a Persian Wheel that is adjacent to a little stream of water. The interior of the building is set up like a desi village, thus contributing the word 'village' to the title. Colored windows, cream-colored walls and an accompanying accordionist add wonders to the place. Hence, a night out at Salt'n Pepper Village is a night to remember.

18. Get Sporty At The Battlefield

When it comes to extreme sports, there aren't many places you would find in Lahore, or Pakistan for that matter, that offer such activities. The Battlefield at Ghazi Road is one of the only zones that offers extreme sports and a number of other similar activities to make your day. The most popular activity at Battlefield is paintball, which is why the place is often called Battlefield Paintball. Paintball packages start at Rs.500 for 25 pellets and lead up to Rs.2000 for 170 pellets, so load up those paintball markers with pellets and shoot away! While you're at it, do try their other popular activities too, like go-karting, quad biking, and bungee trampoline. A day spent at Battlefield will surely be one thrill of a day!

19. Try A Classic Cone At Paradise

Now, this isn't a tip you'll find in any tourist guide; this is a suggestion purely by me. Everyone loves ice cream, regardless of having a sweet tooth or not. You may have eaten hundreds of ice cream flavors from well-known brands like Baskin Robbins, but nowhere will you find a flavor like the one at Paradise, Liberty Market. Paradise offers only one flavor of ice cream: classic vanilla and chocolate mix. This may sound plain and boring but it is lip-smacking tasty. Paradise's cone is the type of ice cream you would get jealous of seeing people eat. If you would like a whole meal instead of skipping to dessert, then worry not! Paradise offers some meticulously prepared street food that is just as good, but not as unforgettable as their ice creams!

20. Catch A Pleasant Breeze At The Shalimar Gardens

Missing out this popular landmark is like forgetting to frost a cake. The Shalimar Gardens were built by the Mughal emperor Shah Jahan and remain immensely popular to this day for their grand architecture and vibrant-hued plantations. The garden complex covers an area of 16 hectares that is encircled by an intricately designed brick wall. They are laid out on three levels of terraces, of which nearly 410 fountains splash water into wide marble pools. Till this date, engineers haven't figured out the exact workings of the water system and the thermal engineering! The Khwabgah or the sleeping chambers of the emperor and his wives and the Sawan Bhadoon pavilions are some of the many notable structures in the Shalimar Gardens. These gardens have a number of multi-purpose buildings like a royal bath, pavilions, grand halls and many others. Plan a picnic and visit the Shalimar Gardens on a pleasant day, with the mindset to relax for the day.

"Lahore was a different world in its own; the busy life, the rich history, the colorful culture, and the unfamiliar faces,"

– Javaria Waseem, In the Shadows of Light at Night

Shehr Naz Ashraf

21. Don't Hold Back On Your Humor

Most tourists choose their words carefully when conversing with locals just to make sure they don't offend them to even the slightest degree. While doing so, most of them completely skip the humorous aspect of things and exempt from making jokes. You can avoid doing that in Lahore. Lahoris have a very vast and entertaining sense of humor and they love to hold witty discussions with others. In fact, the more you warm up to their humor, the more they welcome you. I assure you that locals take jokes easily and never let them get to their heart. Of course, you have to maintain some level of respect for the people's patriotism, but otherwise, when you speak in sarcastic undertones, Lahoris will reply with an equally amusing tone. So the next time you think of a witty response to something, let it out and you will find yourself engaged in the liveliest of conversations.

22. Have A Chill Lassi At Chacha Feeka Lassi To Brighten Up Your Day

Lassi is one desi drink that even foreigners have admitted to adoring. Made from yogurt and water, lassi can be either sweet or savory. The best place to try lassi at would be Chacha Feeka Lassi, also called Fiqay ki Lassi. Located in Gawalmandi Food Street, the place is always packed with so many customers that you now have to take a token and line up in a considerably long queue. It is undoubtedly worth the wait. The place serves absolutely the best lassi in the whole of Lahore. Their peray wali lassi is definitely their trademark and is often described as 'irresistible'. Lassi also has many health benefits, so you might find yourself having a mug a day. Improved digestion, prevention of stomach problems and its role as an energy drink are an added bonus to the yummy drink.

23. Become A Part Of The Horse And Cattle Show At Fortress Stadium

The National Horse and Cattle Show is held annually at Fortress Stadium, in the third week of November. The event lasts for five days, during which livestock farmers from all over the country, as well as tourists and dignitaries from abroad, come together and witness an event that signifies Pakistan's agricultural prosperity. The show is simply uplifting and enthusiastic to watch, especially since the show offers more than just a display of the best breeds of livestock. Polo matches, dog shows, dances by camels and horses and several other entertaining activities will ensure that you have the time of your life at the event. A special performance by foreign groups is always sure to be the highlight of the evening, like the creative use of lights to create intricate patterns at night. The Horse and Cattle Show happens once in a year, but it always makes sure to leave deep impressions on viewers, who cannot help but return another year for another night of pure entertainment!

24. Experience A Throwback Into Mughal Glory At Jahangir's Tomb

A visit to a glorious tomb belonging to the king of a glorious empire would be as magnificent as it sounds. Jahangir's Tomb is one of the most intricately designed and built tombs of the Mughal era, coming second only to the Taj Mahal. The tomb lies in Shahdara Bagh along the banks of the River Ravi. The story behind its construction is a romantic tale, in which Emperor Jahangir's wife Nur Jahan designed and funded the construction at a favorite spot of the couple, the Dilkhusha Garden. Even the entrance of the tomb, which is through the Akbari Sarai, is highly embellished and only leads to areas even more exquisitely designed. A

Persian-style paradise garden surrounds the actual tomb and adds to the splendor of the place. The Emperor's cenotaph lies solely in a beautifully crafted chamber whose beauty cannot be described in words. The tomb is an example of Mughal architecture at its finest, especially because of the Mughals' typical natural light-filtering construction techniques that make the already picturesque scene even more picturesque. While the tombs of Nur Jahan and Jahangir's brother in law, Asif Khan, also stand tall at the Shahdara Bagh, you have to admit that Jahangir's tomb is the ultimate show-stealer.

25. Drive Along The Canal Bank Road

The infamous Lahore Canal acts as Lahore's main artery with its flow between major highways. The 60 km long waterway has been a trademark of Lahore since Mughal rule and has survived even British rule, in spite of the numerous controversies surrounding its water. The Canal is what makes Lahore, Lahore. Although it may seem like a mere water channel to you, it holds great cultural importance. If you drive past the Canal Bank Road on a typical sunny day, you will witness the attachment that people have developed with the canal. Locals relish the canal's cool water in the simmering heat, spend time swimming in the waters and eat watermelons along its banks. You will find women dipping their feet into the water while their kids run around and play enthusiastically. You should go for it, too! This type of warm fun is definitely hard to find. The canal is also worth visiting during national and religious holidays like Independence Day or Eid when it is decorated with bright and colored lights that create a simply stunning scenery.

26. Enjoy Lahore's Nightlife At Liberty Market

Imagine a city where nightlife is a charm itself: a city that just doesn't fall asleep. That's Lahore! Lahore is generally an active and fast-paced city but when it comes to night time, most nocturnal people who stay inside during the day to avoid the intense heat, come out and make up for their absence by keeping the city alive and bustling even at night time. A place to live this phenomenon at is the Liberty Market. The market is a globule of fun and color amidst the dark hues of night time. Shops and businesses of every kind, brands and locals included, are operating with full vigor. You will always find a musician or two who keep the atmosphere alive with their melodious tunes. There are various low-priced eateries in the market that will keep you full with their rich tastes while you look for sales at stores. If you're lucky enough, you may be able to ride horses in the parking lot, an activity that happens every once in a while, but not every day. Getting a firsthand experience of Lahore's nightlife is nothing short of a luxury!

27. Try Nisbat Gol Gappay For A Mouthwatering Snack

Gol gappay is another example of snacks that are popular in all of South Asia. The snack has many variations in its preparation, depending on the location of the chef. A traditional gol gappay dish consists of a fried, crispy vessel that is filled with spicy chanay or yogurt and dipped in both or either one of katha (sour) or meetha (sweet) liquids. You can get gol gappay in many places in Lahore, but no one can beat the taste of Nisbat Gol Gappay. The shop is located at Nisbat Road near Lakshmi Chowk, among a dozen other popular eating spots, yet it still manages to stand out. After getting a taste of this mouthwatering snack, you will realize why gol gappay is one of the most sought after snacks in Lahore.

28. Sit With Lahoris During Cricket Matches

Field hockey may be Pakistan's national game, but it is cricket that all Pakistanis go gaga over. The sport's popularity here is sky high, to say the least. When match season kicks in, Lahoris close down their businesses, prepare bowls of popcorn and get together just to watch the cricket match. Even if every shop in a market has a television, all shopkeepers will gather at only one big shop and enjoy the match while sipping lassi. Families unite near television screens, put on Pakistan's cricket team's t-shirts and paint their faces green and white in support of their country. This kind of unity is the best kind of unity to become a part of. The pure enthusiasm and zeal of Lahoris will amaze and amuse you at the same time, until you, too, become a part of their fervor. The anticipation before the bat hits the ball, the anxiety when the ball flies up high, and the celebratory screams when the team scores a six, are all part of the fervent experience that is cricket.

29. Have A Movie Night At CineStar IMAX

Everyone loves to relax and have a night out from time to time. And what is a better way to relax than watching a movie at a theatre? CineStar IMAX is the first IMAX theatre to open up in Pakistan and is regarded as one of the top 3D movie theatres across the country, despite being launched just in 2014. The cinema is as good as any cinema in the West, which is a big achievement considering Pakistan is a third-world country. The cinema boasts a perfect sound system, huge screens with flawless resolutions, and a snack bar with varieties of snacks to choose from. As if that isn't enough to make watching a movie memorable, CineStar IMAX also allows visitors to enjoy spicy burgers from

Burger King. So whether it is a 3D action tale or an animated feature you want to watch, head straight to CineStar IMAX to have a premium film-watching experience.

30. Spend A Lazy Day At The Jilani Park

Jilani Park is one of the biggest parks in Lahore. With a good jogging track, an artificial lake, and swings and rides of all types, the park is a great place to kill some time at. The place is ideal for morning joggers, who can even enjoy a yoga class held early morning. Jilani Park hosts many festivals and competitions all year round like the horse riding and polo competitions on the polo ground, the annual spring festival in early spring or the Eat Festival for Lahore's foodies. The flower show in early spring is the most popular event hosted at the park. The ceremony begins with folk dances, performances by army bands and acrobatic performances; it goes on to host a beautiful exhibition of all kinds of flowers and plants. The Jilani Park is a great place to destress yourself at and take a fresh breath of air, so visit the park on any lazy day.

"I have grown up listening to my grandparents' stories about 'the other side' of the border. But, as a child, this other side didn't quite register as Pakistan, or not-India, but rather as some mythic land devoid of geographic borders, ethnicity and nationality. In fact, through their stories, I imagined it as a land with mango orchards, joint families, village settlements, endless lengths of ancestral fields extending into the horizon, and quaint local bazaars teeming with excitement on festive days. As a result, the history of my grandparents' early lives in what became Pakistan essentially came across as a very idyllic, somewhat rural, version of happiness."

— *Aanchal Malhotra*

Shehr Naz Ashraf

31. Bond With Wildlife At The Lahore Zoo

You may have visited zoos in your country back when you were a kid, but Lahore's zoo is unlike any other since it is the fourth oldest zoo in the world. The zoo has a collection of 1380 animals of 136 species and 1280 trees of 71 species. Lahore Zoo is a spot that people never miss on their visit to Lahore. The zoo's animal exhibits include the Fancy Aviary for birds, houses for tigers, elephants, giraffes, deer, monkeys, and snakes, and crocodile ponds. While the nation's favorite elephant Suzi is no longer alive to entertain visitors, the zoo has its hippo named Rani, a white rhinoceros, as well as a family of chimpanzees, who are now the most popular animals at the zoo. Some other attractions at the zoo are camel rides, a waterfall and a gift shop sponsored by the WWF. The Lahore Zoo was and still is one of Lahore's most visited destinations for tourists and truthfully, it doesn't disappoint.

32. Switch Your Omelet Up For A Halwa Puri Breakfast At Taj Mahal Sweets

By now, you would have noticed how important of a role food plays in making Lahore, Lahore. But no matter how often you eat at traditional restaurants, you haven't experienced a true Lahori's lifestyle until you have had halwa puri for breakfast. The concept of breakfast at home is alien to typical, traditional Lahoris. There is no such thing as preparing breakfast for the ever-hungry Lahori; Lahoris will go out and have foods like halwa puri, hareesa, and even nihari. The most popular of typical Lahori breakfasts is halwa puri and what better place to eat it than at Taj Mahal Sweets? The shop's owner has been selling halwa puri at Fort Road since 1967 and once you get a taste of his halwa puri, you will definitely see how a dish costing as cheap as Rs.20 could fund this shop's existence since half a century. The sweet taste of halwa paired with spicy chanay and a puri (bread) to scoop all these delicacies – this is the dish responsible for all that buzz!

33. Visit The National Museum Of Science And Technology For An Educational Experience

Lahore is Pakistan's cultural hub for sure, yet most people forget that Lahore has more to offer than just historical sights and rich food. The National Museum of Science and Technology (NMST), located on the Grand Trunk Road, stands proud as one of the most frequented places by students and scholars from all over the country. With four galleries and more than 500 permanent exhibits to offer, the museum makes for one good of an experience. NMST is home to South Asia's largest Foucault pendulum, about 85 feet long and weighing a staggering 110 kilograms. Another amazing exhibit to visit is the Salt Mine, which is designed to replicate the Khewra Salt Mines and make one feel as if they are inside the actual mines. Biotechnology, space, earth sciences – the museum hasn't missed any topic of science, which makes the trip to the place informative as well as memorable.

34. Visit Lahore's Very Own Eiffel Tower

Lahore has its very own Eiffel Tower at Bahria town, which, despite being the replica of a very well-known building, attracts as many people as the actual one in Paris. Just like the actual Eiffel Tower, this one has an elevator to carry you to the top and experience the full glory of being atop a structure 80-feet high. To satisfy visitors' accompanying hunger, there are several restaurants nearby, the most popular one being the L'Eiffel Bistro and Café. The place looks best when visited on a cloudy or slightly rainy day. The building proves to be a pleasant surprise, despite being a replica. On some special holidays, like New Year, the tower is lit up with brilliant, colored light displays and add-on fireworks that further brighten up the atmosphere. A visit to Lahore's very own Eiffel Tower is anything but boring!

35. Shop Like A Lahori At Anarkali Bazaar

One of Lahore's oldest and most popular bazaars, the Anarkali Bazaar is such a huge marketplace that you will need an entire day just to look at all the shops and stores on every single street and alley. The two-hundred-year-old bazaar is situated on the Mall and derives its name from an inspiring history. 'Anarkali' was a courtesan during Mughal Emperor Akbar's time, who was thought to have been ordered to be buried alive by the Emperor because of a love affair between the girl and the Emperor's son, Prince Salim (later called Emperor Jahangir). The bazaar itself has two portions: Old Anarkali and New Anarkali. The former is known for its delicious food items while the latter is renowned for its traditional handicraft and embroidered clothes. Generally, the whole market offers textiles, garments, souvenirs and a ton of other stuff at the lowest rates. The Anarkali Bazaar tops all local markets with its reasonable priced goods. Just don't forget to take cash with you; not many stores accept credit/debit cards! In addition to shopping at the bazaar, you can also visit the picturesque mausoleum of Sultan Qutb ud-Din Aibak, the founder of the Mamluk dynasty.

36. If You Happen To Visit Lahore During Eid Holidays, Then Don't Even Think Of Sitting Back Home

Eid is a religious festival celebrated twice a year, in the Islamic months of Ramadan and Zil Hajj respectively. For Lahoris, the time of Eid is special not just for religious reasons, but for social reasons too. Whether you are a Muslim or a non-Muslim, the day just before Eid, called Chand Raat, is the best day for you to get out and explore local markets. You will spot mehndi and henna stalls at every corner, with significantly long queues of girls waiting for their turns. Jewelry stores will be showcasing their bangle collections as priorities since wearing bangles with traditional clothes is an eternal trend at Eid. Even the biggest of brands will offer sales and discounts on Chand Raat. However, the most convincing reason to get out at this night is the stunning views you will get to see. Every shop, every banner, and some houses even, will be flooded with decorative lights that create some of the most beautiful scenes you will ever witness. So sitting home a day before Eid is an absolute no-no!

37. Do Get A Taste Of Paan

Everyone here is obsessed with paan. And it's for all the right reasons. You'll find a paan shop every few miles and each and every one of them will have at least a dozen customers at all times. Paan is an easy-to-eat snack that consists of areca nuts (and sometimes tobacco too!) wrapped in an edible leaf. You can either chew and spit it out or simply swallow it in. Either way, there is a special sort of satisfaction that only eating paan can grant. Most paanwalas (paan makers) will make their best paans when they spot a foreigner so that's a plus. Also, you can tell when someone's guilty of eating a few paans by their red-hued lips!

38. While Driving, Take A Moment To Check Out The Artistic Development On Roads

Being the capital city of the province of Punjab, there have been numerous efforts to artistically and architecturally develop Lahore. The government of Punjab has collaborated with art schools, painters and sculptors to beautify the city's roads and roundabouts. Lahore's major roundabouts have bright-colored and exotic flower displays and you will always find a couple people relaxing on these roundabouts.

The most notable roundabouts are the Ringroad roundabouts, the Liberty Roundabout and the Chauburji Roundabout, where you can also stop at the Mughal-era building of Chauburji to delve back to the past. Another sight to catch is the street art throughout Lahore. Along many major roads lie the enthusiastically designed walls that street artists and students from art schools have put their being into decorating. Most of them represent Pakistani culture and important figures throughout the country's history. The city is also filled with high-quality sculptures and majestic fountains that further beautify the whole city. All this aesthetic development has made Lahore a city you'll never forget, so do take some time to appreciate the carefully-designed artwork all over the city!

39. Ditch Taxis For Auto-rickshaws And Qingqis

If you want to travel like a true Lahori, then ditch taxis and cars for a traditional rickshaw or qingqi (pronounced ching-chi) at least once during your stay in Lahore. While a rickshaw is the cheapest and arguably the safest form of individual travel for women, a qingqi is more convenient for most. A qingqi is an open rickshaw with seats facing forward and two backward. They offer more space to sit and allow passengers to fully view everything since they are open. You might be a bit ambivalent about getting onto a qingqi, especially when there's traffic, but worry not, for qingqi drivers have an excellent sense of speed and angles. By opting for a rickshaw or qingqi, you will not only travel in style but will also be able to get a better view of the surroundings and normal lifestyles of Lahoris.

40. Watch A Live Cricket Match At Gaddafi Stadium

As mentioned before, Lahoris (and all Pakistanis, in general) are obsessed with cricket. The popularity of cricket in Lahore has attracted international and national cricket teams' interest in holding cricket matches here. The Gaddafi Stadium hosts cricket matches at both national and international levels, with a capacity of about 27,000 spectators. So whether it is a PSL (Pakistan Super League) match or a World Series match in Lahore, you know where to go. Also, during PSL matches, just remember that Lahore's team is called the 'Lahore Qalandars'. On a side note, most Lahoris root for teams other than Lahore, too, so don't be surprised to find Lahoris who prefer Islamabad's team over Lahore's.

Shehr Naz Ashraf

"Goodbye Lahore, you've been a kind friend."

– Kanza Javed, Ashes, Wine and Dust

Shehr Naz Ashraf

41. Get Intellectual At The Lahore Literary Festival

The Lahore Literary Festival is an annual festival held in Lahore for typically three consecutive days and this literary festival is one that unites writers, scholars, and speakers from Pakistan *and* abroad. The event features discussions and question and answer sessions on politics, literature and art, history and a variety of other topics. The event cultivates a series of intellectually stimulating discussions and interactive debates that liven up the audience. At a given time slot, at least three different programs are arranged to happen, so you can go for one which is a session in English. The Lahore Literary Festival is a great way to experience erudite interactions and mix-ups between cross-cultures, so do give it a shot!

42. Don't Deprive Yourself Of Phajjay Ke Paye

Your visit to Lahore is incomplete if you haven't tried out Phajjay ke Paye. Phajjay is actually the owner's name, not the restaurant's name! The restaurant is called Fazl-e-Haq and while it offers many scrumptious and amazingly cheap desi dishes, its specialty is its paye – lamb trotters. Located at Heera Mandi, the place is one of those spots people flock to every morning to have a greasy yet worthwhile breakfast of paye. The food is spicy enough to enjoy but is generally considered mild as compared to other spicy foods in Lahore, so you can surely handle its taste. If you're up for it, try the restaurant's maghaz (goat brain), khad (jawbone) or zubaan (tongue) too. But the rule of thumb is: never miss out on Phajjay ke Paye!

43. Get Thrilled At Joyland

Lahore has many events and activities for the calm and serene, but where does one go for the thrills? Joyland, of course. The amusement park is located in Fortress Stadium and has been the Six Flags of Pakistan since it opened. The place is suitable for people of all ages so it is equally popular among kids, teenagers, and adults. You can either buy individual rides' tickets which range from Rs.20 to Rs.60, or go for the wristwatch priced at Rs.300 and enjoy as many rides as you want to. For adrenaline junkies, Top Spin, Crazy Boat, and Discovery would be major attractions while kids usually opt for the Tea Cups, Carousel or the gaming center. Dodgem Cars, the Haunted House, and the Flying Carpet are fan favorites. It goes without saying that you should go there on an empty stomach to avoid throwing up. Besides, the place has a canteen offering various refreshing snacks that can revitalize your spirits. Alternatively, you can eat in one of the many restaurants in Fortress Stadium and even opt for a movie night or shopping date at the stadium's cinemas and malls.

44. For The Cheapest Rates, Visit Kareem Block Market

If you're short on money and still need to shop, then Kareem Block Market is the perfect place for you. Located in Allama Iqbal Town, the market is just the right place to visit when you are on a budget but need to buy high-quality items. Mobile markets offering affordable smartphones, salons offering facials at the lowest rates and brands' factory outlets selling clothes at half the original price, are some of the most memorable features of Kareem Block Market. The recent addition of well-made roads leading to the market have made access much easier, hence the place now gets frequented by dozens of people daily. If you come across a price tag that reads too high, then good news: sellers here are open to negotiations on their products, so it will always play out in your favor if you try bargaining on items.

45. Fly Through Lahore's Skies With The Lahore Flying Club

The city of Lahore is one of the brightest and most vibrant cities on the planet. What better way to experience Lahore's splendid views than from the skies themselves? With grand historical structures dating back to the Mughal period and modern highways and flyovers emerging from every corner, the aerial view of the city is unparalleled to any other. The Lahore Flying Club is a prestigious aviation institution at the Walton Airport, which allows people to get on a plane and fly over the city for about 20 minutes. The rates are reasonable, with Rs.5000 charged per person. The one thing to remember when booking your flight is to check the weather and security conditions since flights are scheduled only in accordance with these two factors. This joyride is a once in a lifetime experience, so do not miss this!

46. Don't Leave Out The Javed Manzil When Visiting Lahore

The Javed Manzil was the house of the Poet of the East, Dr. Allama Mohammad Iqbal, who is also Pakistan's much-valued national poet. The idea of Pakistan was his brainchild. He has written exceptional poetry in both Urdu and Persian. His white colonial-style bungalow, with its remarkable garden, was converted into a museum by the Pakistan government. All of Iqbal's belongings and furniture have been left as they were in 1938 when he passed away. There are several galleries in the museum displaying his wardrobe, pictures from his lifetime and a room consisting of all his historical documents and papers. A notable item on display is the prayer rug on which Iqbal offered his prayers at the grand mosque of Cordoba, Spain. However, nothing beats the room in the house's far left corner: Iqbal's personal space, where he passed away early in the morning on April 21, 1938. The room is haunting, to say the least. The air of death hasn't left the little room since the sad day of Iqbal's demise. Everything is in the same position as it was that day: the unmade bed covering, his slippers placed beside the bed and the date on the calendar – April 21, 1938. The Javed Manzil, which literally means 'house of eternity', will always be an eternally mystifying landmark to visit.

47. Check Out Kamran's Baradari At The Shahdara Bagh

A Baradari is a typical Mughal pavilion with three doorways on each side of the square-shaped structure. This gives a total of twelve doors to the pavilion, which relates it to the word 'baradari'; 'bara' means twelve and 'dar' means 'door' in Urdu. Kamran's Baradari is attributed to Prince Mirza Kamran, son of Babur, the first Mughal emperor, and is known to be the oldest Mughal structure in Lahore, dating back to 1540. The pavilion's location is lovely: right in the middle of an island on the River Ravi. The downside to this is that it has been subject to flooding in previous centuries, but its frequent reconstruction has resulted in its current pleasing form. There isn't much to do here if you're looking for some action, but it is definitely the right place to go to if you're interested in visiting age-old heritage sites.

48. Stop By The Grand Jamia Masjid At Bahria Town To View Extraordinary Splendor

The Grand Jamia Masjid at Bahria Town is one of Lahore's finest mosques that is also credited for being the world's seventh largest mosque, with a capacity of 70,000 worshippers. This mosque is unique because it is not a construction of the Mughal era, but a structure of modern days. The mosque holds 4 million handcrafted mosaic tiles, 50 chandeliers straight from Iran and carpets from Turkey. While the Islamic heritage museum in the mosque is a major attraction for Muslims, you can always opt for marveling at the splendid architecture of the building: soaring minarets, vividly colored tile mosaic art and intricate frescoes. The chef-d'oeuvre of the place is the Center Dome, which adds the sought-after majestic touch to the mosque. The up-sides to this grand structure are that it is always open and it is possible to visit the place in any weather. This mosque is a brilliant reminder that Lahore is the city of the past, the present and the future.

49. Free Your Soul At The Mela Chiraghan

A worth-visiting festival celebrated in Lahore is the Mela Chiraghan – festival of lights, which is suitable for the 'city of lights'. The three-day celebration is to mark the death anniversary of Sufi Saint Hazrat Shah Hussain and takes place at the shrine of Shah Hussain at Baghbanpura. The festival features a huge bonfire fed by candles, oils and lit up cotton lamps; people throw in these things hoping to get their wishes and desires fulfilled. Fire torching, lighting candles and the recitation of qawwalis are integral parts of the event. Swings, puppet shows, and magic shows keep children busy while devotees shower rose petals onto the saint's grave. This spiritual festival is more of a soul-cleanser, really. Just be prepared to meet a crowd of the saint's followers that are from places other than Lahore.

50. Elders Who Tell Stories Are A Definite Source Of Entertainment

If you find some elders who can speak English, ask them to tell you stories. Chances are, they'll tell you a story about partition and their family's migration to Pakistan. The chances of refusal are almost zero. In Lahore, everyone has a story to tell. We Lahoris may be wild and crazy but we have soft spots for tragic love stories and miserable tales of migration. Moreover, because of our knack for drama, we tell stories in the most amusing way possible. And coupled with the in-built wit every Pakistani seems to possess, you'll find yourself either splitting your sides with laughter or bathing in a pool of tears at the stories that you will get to hear. Of course, elders are not the only people you will find that have stories to tell, but they usually have the best stories and plenty of free time in which to conjure up entertaining sagas.

Generally, a story is an experience passed down from generation to generation. Every story features some ritual, architecture, food or cultural deed that becomes a suggestion for a tourist. What I'm saying is, these fifty tips are not the end of it. Every story is the continuation of another story you heard from maybe an ancestor, or even a stranger! So go ahead, listen to stories and then make up your own stories to tell!

Top Reasons to Book This Trip

- **Culture**: The vivid and lively culture.

- **Food**: The exceptional tastes will render you speechless.

- **Heritage**: The richest of heritage.

Shehr Naz Ashraf

> TOURIST

GREATER THAN A TOURIST

Visit GreaterThanATourist.com
http://GreaterThanATourist.com

Sign up for the Greater Than a Tourist Newsletter
http://eepurl.com/cxspyf

Follow us on Facebook:
https://www.facebook.com/GreaterThanATourist

Follow us on Pinterest:
http://pinterest.com/GreaterThanATourist

Follow us on Instagram:
http://Instagram.com/GreaterThanATourist

Shehr Naz Ashraf

> TOURIST

GREATER THAN A TOURIST

Please leave your honest review of this book on Amazon and Goodreads. Thank you.

We appreciate your positive and negative feedback as we try to provide tourists guidance on their next trip from a local.

Our Story

Traveling is a passion of the "Greater than a Tourist" series creator. Lisa studied abroad in college, and for their honeymoon Lisa and her husband toured Europe. During her travels to Malta, an older man tried to give her some advice based on his own experience living on the island since he was a young boy. She was not sure if she should talk to the stranger but was interested in his advice. When traveling to some places she was wary to talk to locals because she was afraid that they weren't being genuine. Through her travels, Lisa learned how much locals had to share with tourists. Lisa created the "Greater Than a Tourist" book series to help connect people with locals. A topic that locals are very passionate about sharing.

Shehr Naz Ashraf

Notes

Manufactured by Amazon.ca
Bolton, ON